The Hoodie

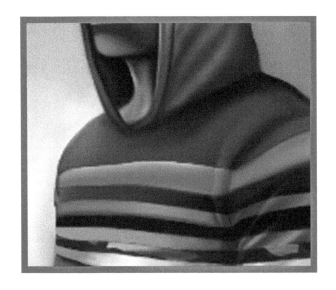

Author
Dr. Sharon F. Shrum

Illustrator
Sandy Woodward

ISBN # Paperback: 979-8-9896142-9-5
ISBN # Hardback: 979-8-9899147-0-8
ISBN eBook: 979-8-9896142-8-8

If you have a teen in your life, go hug them.
Tell them you love them every single day.
Enjoy watching them grow up.
Listen to them.

Let them be who they are.

"No one ever made a difference by being like everyone else."
~ P. T. Barnum

Dedication

To my beautiful children, Desi, Shelbi, and Robbie.
You are my everything. May you never give up and always know
it is better to serve than to receive.

Thank you to my best friend, my husband, Rob.
Thanks for always believing in me.

In honor of my mom, Emma Jean Dawson and my father,
Willie Richard Dawson. As I get older I am all too aware that
material things really don't matter. What you two gave me is exactly
what I needed to survive and prosper in this world.

Most of all I could not do anything without God. HE leads me
and guides me and never gives up on me. I thank him daily.

Table of Contents

The Hoodie
Why I hide

Black hoodie, blue hoodie, red hoodie, white,

--camouflage hoodie, rainbows so bright.

So many hoodies in plain sight?

Wear them in the spring, summer, winter, and fall.

Short people, tall people, white, tan, black, and all.

What do they mean?

Do they stand for something?

Why are people scared?

Why are there rules behind wearing a hoodie?

A garment no different than what people wore in ancient times from monks to nuns to priests to even people back in ancient Greece.

Chapter One
The Black Hoodie (Anxiety)

BLACK

HOODIE

I get up in the morning and I see it sitting there. At the edge of my bed, it glares.

I wear the same one every day, but then again, who cares?

I roll out of bed because I have to, they said, but this is one thing I dread.

I pull it on, over my head, feeling like I can't see.

It has to be loose and makes me feel like I am swimming around in a big black sea.

I bring the hood up over my head and down close to my eyes.

It's large and **black**, no words on the back.

I can barely see, which makes me believe that I am invisible and free.

It hides my face, my body, my soul, and allows no one to know.

The pain I feel, deep inside, to hide and not be real is a feeling that I have come to know.

No one can see me. I hide behind the cloth.
It's so big, it's so warm, but I feel so lost.

I wait for the bus. The cars ride by.
I can feel their eyes upon me, but no one says hi.

I get on the bus. I walk to the back.
I sit down where no one is at.

My knees shake as they bounce up and down, I notice a stare and
try not to care.

I wring my hands under the cuffs of my hoodie.
I feel as though my wrists are bound.

My eyes are down.
They shift back and forth letting no one know who I am, no words,
no sounds.

I try looking up but I keep staring down. It's hard to make sure no
one is around.

The bus is lit but it's still dark outside, why must we get up so early,
just to sit for this ride?

For another forty-five minutes, I ride in
silence even though people are around.

I drown out the noise with earbuds in, eyes
shut, head laid back, and feelings bad in
my gut.

The research says we need more sleep, but
who is reading it, and making changes, no
one says a peep.

It's been out for years, they keep saying it,
but no one changes it.

Do they know how we feel?

The bus stops and pulls with a jerk, we all get up and move slowly to begin our work.

Here we go, another day…

  …off the bus, into school, this is not cool.

I walk into school, I don't want to be seen.

Deep inside I want to be normal. I hate this feeling that I feel.

I just want to think, I want to feel, I want to see.

Why can't they see how dark it is in my head? How nervous I get, how sick I feel.

How I just want to climb inside this hoodie and never return.

That's it– it's the end of the line.
I have to get off the bus.

Slowly moving with all of the rest of the kids I wonder who has these thoughts in their head.

I walk down the steps hoping not to hurl but I am past that now.
I am hurting inside.
  I don't know why I feel this way.

Why can't I be like others and just walk inside?

With a smile on my face and nothing to fear. Why do I feel like I am filled with tears?

The school doors are open. I keep putting one foot in front of the other.

I swear I am doing my best but I am not like the rest.

My face feels like it's on fire. My body aches from head to toe. How can I do this when no one knows?

I've got a plan-I know who can help. I am going to the nurse but I need to go past the office, down the dark hall, maybe none will be there at all.

Okay, I made it into her office. I look around and she's not there.

A woman who I have never met just looks at me and says "what's wrong with you-it's too early for this!"

The feelings inside my stomach get worse.

She doesn't know me. I feel like I am cursed.

She is a substitute getting through the day, she doesn't understand who I am, she just wants to get paid.

My stomach aches like I am going to throw up.

She never says it but I feel like she wants me to just suck it up.

"Go back to class, no fever, no vomit."

Doesn't she realize these symptoms I feel can't be seen on the outside but they are real?

She thinks I am lying but has to call home. I know no one will answer. I feel all alone.

My mom and dad are at work. I know they care but they are so busy they are unaware.

My breaths are getting shorter and my heart is beating faster.

She is going to send me away without any answers.

Every day's the same thing. I wish this feeling would go away but it just seems to stay.

She turns to me and says no one is home, gives me a cracker, a sip of water, and sends me back to class.

I turn away from her and she doesn't say goodbye. It's another day of living a lie.

I take a big breath and feel so confused. My head is spinning. I am in a muse.

My thoughts are on repeat spinning through my head. How can I get rid of this feeling I said?

Self-talk–Self-talk, remember what to do…
——Take a deep breath…
    —Count to ten…
        —Close your eyes and begin again…
        —One foot in front of the other, you got this they say
    You can do it, you know the way.

I keep repeating these things in my head–I got it, I can do it, don't give up, and before you know it I am in front of the classroom door.

So I take another breath and walk in slowly staring at the floor.

When I go into the room everyone is talking.
I slowly slip by people and sit in my seat.

Another hour passes, not sure what is happening, another defeat.

No one is doing a thing, no purpose, no thought, just another day.

I ask myself why are we all here
　　—there is nothing to say.

Another day, please make it real. Why must this be so surreal?

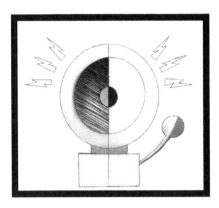

The bell finally rings—
We are all on the move.
Gathering our things
and moving along.

Here we come
　　–black hoodie,
　　–red hoodie,
　　–white hoodie,
　　　　–blue.

We keep moving along, down the halls, around the corner.
　　–can these days be any longer?
The reality is it doesn't have to feel this way, there are others like me
can you see?

Here we are, all the same, we want to be connected,
　　　　–and most of all be respected.
Our feelings are real!
　　We are not making it up! Believe us, stand up for us, we don't
know how to feel.

We want to talk, we want to think, we want to make decisions that
mean more than a worksheet, multiple choice test, a haiku, what a
waste.

Don't you see us?
Help us connect, see us all, know how we feel, and help us
stand tall.

Help us breathe a sigh of relief.

Notice me, notice me I scream in silence, but you see me only as defiance.
I try not to be rude every day but it's about that time when I need to flee. I need to go to the nurse. I have had all that I can stand.
My heart feels like it is going to explode, my hands are sweaty, my stomach hurts and these are all real feelings that are so strong.

My teacher thinks I am faking it.

She shrugs her shoulders and points to the door.

She lets out a frustrated sigh and never says goodbye…
—hope you feel better,
    —c'est la vie,
        —adiós,
            —or just bye.

It's after lunch and I still feel sick so I go back to the nurse to just get away.

Into her office here I go again but it is the regular nurse who's back, she seems almost like a friend. She looks up from her glasses and says how are you doing? I heard you were here this morning.
It must be a hard day but I am glad you went to class and gave it a chance. Come sit for a while, it will pass.

I have been coming here for a while and today is different.

She lets me sit there and we talk about her weekend and she asks what I did during mine.

I didn't know what to say. But I told her I played video games, played with my dog, and read a book.

She asked another question or two. She always seems to know what to do.

She asked what the book was about and I told her it was a history book with lots of facts.

She said she liked history and she liked the facts-everything seemed straightforward and intact.

Before I knew it an hour had passed and she said how are you feeling? I said "better, thanks".

She asked if I wanted to try and go back or did I wanted to hang out there with her and the other kids who came in and went out.

I said I will go back to class. It's history, we both laughed and said "I think I can last."

As I walk down the hall, the bell rings, and we all move again.

Like herds of cattle from one place to the end.

I sit down way in the back, looking up a little but not past the other guys' back.

I like listening to the stories in this class and thinking about who I would be if I lived in the past.

It's at least interesting and different from the rest of the classes.

My teacher stays up front and talks a lot but she shows us pictures and videos and more. I feel like I am learning and never get bored.

The feeling creeps into me again, I am getting anxious for no reason I try not to let it in.

She never comes near, she never comes close. She only stares. I wonder, are you aware?

Do you have something to fear?
Can you not see my tears? I wipe it away so no one sees, the hood protects me, and it makes it easy to breathe. I can do this, I can do this. I say to myself.

You get closer. What is going on? My heart is racing. I hear it in my head, faster and faster it goes.
Thump, thump, thump, thump, thump, thump, thump…

The clicking of your heels comes to a stop.

You were close enough, I thought.

Please don't talk to me or ask me a question.

I don't want to be here, be embarrassed, no connection.

I raised my head, because it was silent. Your eyes caught mine and we could not look away.

Today was different…
… you looked at me but I didn't look away.
You smiled a little and I smiled back.

You didn't ask me anything, you just moved away. Maybe you could see I wasn't ready for you to be that close that day.

It reminded me of a time when I found stray kittens. Every day I would feed them and they would run away.
But after a week or so I put the food out, they came close to me but I could not move or they would run without a doubt.

I would do this every day and I would get closer and even talk out loud just talking to them to see if they would stay.
One day I reached out and touched them each when they were eating their food but could not see my hand coming.

Gently touching and quietly talking they began to trust me and soon crawled all over me and around me.

Just like you, you come near, I feel you look down.

You bend down beside me, my heart races fast.

I start to breathe heavily, but so no one hears, I can hear my heart in my head, why do I feel this I said.

Again and again, each day goes by I am getting less scared deep inside.

And then one day you softly said hi.

You were close to my desk.

I had to respond.

There was no getting out of this.

Is this a test?

Then, nothing more, nothing less, not a sound or a peep.

She walked away slowly while I sit
in my seat.
I come back the next day, again, and again and I notice you see me
and talk every day.

About this or about that, you always say something. I barely
speak back.

You ask me a question, how was my day?' I replied without fear this
time, "it was ok."

It's like you want me to talk.

I feel less anxious and begin to share.

Not just a few words but coherent thoughts. This is weird.

My heart slows down when I walk into your class because I know
what to expect.

It's not like before. You come over to me and we talk out loud for
all to see.

I am not afraid to look up and you are not afraid to say hi.

Maybe it's just as hard for you to
see your why.

You have been around for a long time, they say.

I guess we have changed since you began in
your day.

I never thought about your feelings, your stress, your thoughts.

It took all I had to deal with mine I thought.

I think we are all still the same, we just need time to connect and not have shame.

Your class is different.

It's not like the rest.

You make things relevant even on the test.

Your questions are real and cause us to think.

You share your point of view and respect us

all, too.

There is never any sarcasm, no jokes, and poking fun. Just high expectations and a little fun.

Thanks for believing in me no matter where I am from, expecting the same things, and not making fun. You got to know me and I know you better too. I wish all teachers could be just like you.

I get up in the morning and see my hoodie over there. I think for a second I need to be me.

I leave it home today and go on my way.

I feel accepted and respected, I don't need you today.

I have come so far, I can stand tall, without my hoodie every day, I do have a say.

I had to find my strength, my space, my way, and this all happened because of you.

The time you took was different from others.

You didn't demand, yell, or say get out.

You didn't believe what you heard about me.

You got to know me.

What I dreamed of, what I felt.

You cared about me and not what others had said.

Why can't all teachers do this, I wonder?

Take time and figure us out, help us be ourselves and not shout.

Our hoods are on because we need help.

We are young and full of doubt.

We are not always nice but it's a front to make you think we have it figured out.

I hadn't visited the nurse in a while and soon I didn't feel like I needed to because something changed deep inside.

I am getting less anxious. I am going to be fine.

Every day is a fight that I am determined to win. Sure makes it easier when you have a friend.

My teacher and the nurse may not be my friends but they are nice, kind, and patient and I don't feel so behind.

I made it through the class. I learned a little, I hope it lasts. My teacher connected to me today and I was nervous at first but then it soon went away.

I am a little excited about coming here tomorrow. It has been the highlight of my day.

Fact: *Banana Moon makes a hoodie to help people with anxiety. The Hoodie has several sensory tools such as a tactile infinity circle, fidget, weighted pockets, and more.*

https://www.banana-moon-clothing.co.uk/personalised-clothing/unisex/hoodies/anti-anxiety-hoodie-2584

Children with anxiety need to have time to move through their emotions. Abraham Maslow's hierarchy of needs is a theoretical model that explains the understanding of human behavior. Part of the hierarchy is the feeling of love and belonging, a sense of connection. The more we build positive relationships with students and get to know them the more they will see their inner potential. Maslow refers to this as self-actualization when a person experiences purpose, acceptance, and can become creative and spontaneous.

Strategies like deep breaths, counting, tapping and so on can help to get a person to relax in order to be able to make good decisions but connections and relationships that show the person they are needed and valued have a positive long-lasting impact. Allowing students to have their hoods up doesn't cost or hurt anyone but not taking the time to understand why the hood up can cause a lot of pain for the student. Harassing the student to remove the hood again causes the person not to feel loved or belonging. Helping students build self-esteem, confidence, and feel valued are all important components of human behavior. Benjamin Bloom, researcher of student achievement. Many times in a school setting we are worried about how to move the students forward in their learning but as the old saying goes we need to "Maslow before we Bloom." In other words, we need to fulfill the basic needs of love and safety before we can think about academics.

Chapter Two
The Blue Hoodie (ADHD)

BLUE

HOODIE

I see a **blue hoodie** across the room.

It is pulled down over his eyes.

He is tall and thin, a face without a grin.

Eyes are shifting back and forth but never really looking up, just one

more lost pup.

As he sits in the seat, his pen is clicking, to a specific beat.

The sound of his knees bouncing up
and down, hand up against the desk and on the ground.

Moving back and forth in the seat, he can't sit still, the teacher says
"hey you, over there" to get his attention.

"You need to stop, stop and listen."

He buries himself deep in his hood, finally, he can't stay still so he
gets up and shoves his desk to the side and out the door, he spills.

The next day he begins again. He tries so hard to sit still and not
click his pen.

His hands begin to shake as I ask the students to write about some
random 1865 Pope.

As I glance over at him, I am wondering if he is going to do something today.

I see no words on his paper but he begins to move his pen.

Back and forth the pen moves faster.

Almost like he is not even thinking but then when I look over again and see beautiful designs all over the page, faces, hands, and figures begin to appear.

He is drawing the pope, in his garb and skull cap making speech bubbles that answer the essay question more profoundly than just words on a page.

The teacher collects the papers at the end of class and when she gets to him she picks up his paper, she stares in awe.

She had no idea she was doing this wrong.

The teacher thought to herself,
    "why didn't I see what he had to offer?"
      "I thought he didn't care, what was I after?"

She looked at him with a puzzled look on her face and a twinkle in her eyes– "I know what you need now, it's me–I need to change to open up your sky."

She was so thankful that he drew his thoughts out on paper that she shared his work aloud.

The excitement in her voice changed that day as she showed the class the beautiful drawings that explain his thinking she shared, who else would like to use illustrations to show their thinking?

A few brave souls raised their hands and she said yes to each and they began to draw.

A few other students asked, "Can I build a model?"

"Can I work with a partner?"

"Can I write a song?"

She said, "Yes, Yes, and Yes to all!" I just need to know that you understand it all. No more multiple-choice tests unless you prefer, I want to know each one of you and how you think.

I don't want to miss a word, a picture, or a song. Let's start over and we will all get along.

She began to share with his permission and you could see his eyes beginning to show.

From beneath the hood, his confidence began to grow.

As the teacher shared her interpretation of his work he could see that she believed in him and he thought maybe this could work.

She shared, "I can see the details in the pope's face, his crown looks so real, it's all in place."

"You did it!"

"This is amazing!"

How could I not know you? She thought.

Now her hands were shaking.

She feels so bad.

How have I failed?

What have I done?

How can I change and notice who they are?

I need to get to know each and every star.

That is just it, **they are all stars**.

Not just the ones who raise their hand high in the air, who speak out loud for all to hear.

He enters my room every day.

I need to get to know him better and I need to do better.

Today is the day I make the change.

I didn't begin with vocabulary and all of the facts or show them a movie and a bunch of other crap.

I had to get real and meet them halfway.

I had high expectations and believed in them in every way.

I gave them a choice.

They debated and discussed.

Some wrote, some painted, some made things 3-D.

As long as they understood the concepts it was fine by me.

The room became full of life. I could explain what happened.

I began to understand them.

I believed in them.

I cared about each and every one of them.

They changed my life.

I needed to engage them and show them I cared.

It all changed for all of them but especially for the blue hood.

I am amazed at how his hand stopped shaking, his hood went down, he even made a few jokes with others and began to fit in.
He uses his talent to represent his thoughts and I gave him the avenue to be true to himself.

He began to believe in himself, smile, laugh, and enjoy the class.

Others tell him how amazing he is.

As he gets going, the images he draws pour out like paint on a canvas wall.

I am amazed at just how far we both have come.

I am glad we both kept learning, took time to know each other, and had some fun.

Fact: Meditation is one coping strategy to help people with ADHD.

Having a hoodie on can help stop distractions and allow students to meditate without seeing so many things in their peripheral vision.

Allowing students to move, to stand up, a yoga ball or wide elastic bands on the bottom of their chair can help with the constant motion that needs to exist.

The more that students who have ADHD move the better the working memory performs. Someone once told me that having ADHD is like your brain being on a very fast motor and your body is constantly trying to fight to keep it in check. You have difficulty paying attention because of this inner struggle. Then to layer on the impulsiveness and restlessness that is occurring at the same time is sometimes unbearable.

Movement helps with being alert and responsive because it releases a natural dopamine that increases neurotransmitters and allows the brain to improve focus and alertness. Sometimes we need to change our behavior and the environment to enable our students to reach their fullest potential.

Chapter Three
The Red Hoodie (Autism)

 HOODIE

We enter another classroom. It's loud and bright. Lights are flickering in my sight.

My red hoodie is pulled tightly down over my face. I can see just enough, and I really need some space.

My hands are cupped tightly over my ears, trying to stop the sounds, the light, the noise, and most of all my fears.

I sit down at my desk, and it's too cold, too hard, too small, too tall. I start rocking back and forth, feeling their eyes all upon me.

The room is getting louder and smaller with all of the students rushing in. I can't do this again and so it begins.

The teacher says so many things while writing on the board, when I try to advocate for myself, I only get ignored.

I feel myself moving back and forth with my hands on my ears but it doesn't make it stop.

It's so hard to get help and attention. I just want to do well.

But they either stare or avoid me and hope that I don't yell.

The teacher is distracted and doesn't know what to do–
— so she reaches out for help but today is another loss too.

Why can't they see me? Don't they understand? I am not trying to be disruptive or take a stand.

The next day the teacher comes into the classroom with a friend. The class gets noisy and here we go again.

My teacher introduces her to the class and she says she is a BCBA. I don't know what that means but I hope she doesn't stay.

She sits in the back of the room and watches us like pets in a zoo. I look back at her and see that she is watching me too.

Who is this new person? Is she a friend or a foe?
Is she someone I can trust or is it just another bust?

I begin to rock but I notice the BCBA kneeling down beside me. She holds something out that I can't quite see.

It's a neat pair of headphones without any wires. She smiles and says "Do you want to try these? They may help to be a sound modifier."

I slide them on over my hoodie but she asks me to take the hoodie down so they will cut out all of the sound.

She had a few pairs, and said "Choose which ones you would like for school!"

Of course, I choose the red ones because they look cool.

I look over at her and I can do my work and she smiles.
We talk about a signal when the teacher is talking and then I can put them back on for a while.

She checked in again when the class was over and said "How do you do in the halls?" It's really hard to keep it together. I have to fight it but it's like hitting a wall.

I told her that I would like to try them in the hall because lots of kids wear headphones, she said "That's great! You'll definitely not be alone."

I still don't know what a BCBA is but I am doing better and so are my teachers.

I feel like I can follow all of their procedures!

No more bursting out and I can finally lower my hood, I fit in now and I feel understood.

Fact: Many children who are diagnosed with autism can experience sensory sensitivities and become overloaded by stimuli, but when wearing their hoodie up they can block out bright lights and busy environments which helps to calm them and regain their focus. Using cool colors in the classroom, avoiding clutter on the walls, and around the room can also help.

Specific visuals to support the students as reminders located on their desks or pictures that can be used to shorten long explanations will help support our learners. Leaving routines and schedules posted on the wall can help when another teacher needs to fill in for the teacher.

Autism falls under a wide spectrum of disorders called Pervasive Developmental Disorders (PDD) or Autism Spectrum Disorder (ASD). Therefore, just because something works for one child does not mean it will work for another. Families know their child best and working with the families as a teacher you can create a team that allows you both to understand and know what supports are best.

The words for this story come from interviewing several students and hearing what they have gone through. Parents, teachers, and community members can educate children to understand that we are all different and we sometimes need different things. We need to teach our children that when it comes down to it we are all different. Different doesn't mean bad.

Thank you to all of my brave children who talked openly and shared their stories with me.

Chapter Four
The Gray Hoodie (Poverty)

GRAY

HOODIE

I just got up, I am running late. Run to the bus wearing the same clothes I had on for the last three days. Hoping no one notices. I run up the street to catch the bus that never slows down long enough to see what is going on. My sister is running behind me and when I arrive at the next stop I tell the bus driver to hold her horses because my sister is coming.

She looks at me with a glare on her face. Mumbling under her breath "why do I put up with this?"

Seats are all full but one person gets up as I am approaching the seat and they get up and move leaving me the whole seat. I think to myself, fine, whatever, just leave me alone.

As I am sitting on the long ride to school with my face against the window, I wonder what will happen today when I get home. Who will be in the house or will I be all alone?

When I walked out the door Mom was in bed, not a goodbye, not a smile, or even a nod of the head. Who knows what time she came home last night. The house was a wreck with dishes piled high. Roaches crawling over the plates and on the day-old pie.

When I walk into my house each day it is so unlike the place where I can think, learn, and play. When I go to school the rooms are clean, the water runs warm, and there is food where I don't have to pay.

I wander into class and the first thing she says is "hood down in this room! And I don't want any sass!"

I start to walk on by her and she grabs the back of my hood, yanks it so hard my head jerks back. I am in disbelief. I don't understand, I am doing the best that I can.

I don't even sit down. I turn quickly back around. I go to the office where I feel most wanted and respected and I look for the principal. She cares and always has a smile. She said good morning and asked how was my day, or was everything ok? I don't know why it seems no one else does. To be honest I wish she were my mom sometimes. My mom has been through a lot and does her best but the drugs, alcohol, and her guy friends are not what is best.

My principal said to me have you had breakfast, I said no and she handed me a breakfast bar. I hurriedly eat it and she says get another and then continues to talk to me as though I am not a bother. I am so hungry and she sees me looking at the basket that is full of breakfast bars in every flavor you can imagine. She says take a few and put them in your pocket so you can have some tonight when you need a snack.

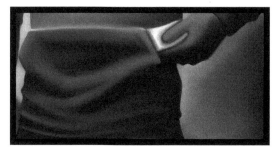

I thought to myself, this is supper for me and my sister, it's not a snack like she thinks. I take a few and put them in the pocket of my hoodie and I hold them tight as she continues to talk. She tells me about her boys and you can tell she loves them so much. I wish I could go home with her and be in a nice clean house. With food in the refrigerator and everyone was happy. Not wondering when your mom was coming home and your stomach growling all night long.

She asked me what happened because she had to answer a phone call while I was in her office and I knew it was the teacher. I could hear the whole thing. I told her I had just walked in and she pulled my hood down. I said I know I was not supposed to have it up because I am not able to brush my hair. I couldn't find a hairbrush and I had to run out the door, and I was going to take it down after I went to the bathroom to wash my face and wet my hair. We didn't have shampoo and no hot water so I have not been able to take a bath until we get it fixed. The apartment owner won't fix it until mom pays the rent but she took all the money she had and bought paint and some brushes for her artwork that she says she is going to sell.

I was talking so fast because I had her attention and I didn't want the teacher to say I was just being defiant. I really am trying and doing my best but I am just a kid and I am not like the rest.

The principal just looks at me with tears in her eyes. She doesn't know what to say and I see her turn away. She wiped her face quickly and turned back to me and she said, let's go get some breakfast and we are going to have a good day.

I finish my breakfast and she sits with me and has breakfast too. I still don't know why she cares about me but I am glad she does. She takes me to a closet that is full of clothes and food and she says to pick something out that fits. Grab some underwear and socks and see if there are any shoes and put your clothes in the bag and I will give them back to you after school.

I go and change and give her my bag of dirty clothes. She says there is a hairbrush and deodorant over there, go grab one for you and your sister. She made up a book bag full of supplies and she said I will have something ready for you at the end of the day when you come by.

I told her thank you and walked over to her and just hugged her for caring so much. She didn't say a word, she hugged me so tight. She then said you are going to have a good day. You have everything you need. Go back to class and I will be down in a while. I need to check on something but I will see you soon.

She goes one way and I go the other. As soon as I sit down, the telephone rings in the room, and in walks the assistant principal. My teacher walked out and the assistant principal shared that my teacher would be back soon and that the principal needed to see her.

I sit down in my chair and begin to work on the paper in front of me. It is a test and I do my best but I am not sure I can pass. I try to study on the way home on the bus because that is the only time I have. I get home and no one is there, so I go outside to play with some older guys from the middle school who are kind of cool.

Sometimes they have food and they share. It gets dark and their moms call them in and I am always hoping they ask me to come for supper but most times that's a dead end.

I walk back to the apartment, with the streetlights lighting the way to see if my sister made it home. She is already in bed. I can hear her whimpering and crying herself to sleep. Mom is not home and she can't sleep. I walk into her room and pull out a breakfast bar for her. I told her everything was going to be ok and I had another breakfast bar for her in the morning. I hugged her and she went off to sleep.

I don't even know what the day will bring, but I know I can always count on my principal. It's not just me she cares about. She cares about all kids. She gives me a bag of food on Fridays that we can usually stretch over the whole weekend. I know most kids probably like school because of their friends or their teacher but I like school because it's warm, it's clean, it's safe, and it's consistent. I like school because they care.

I usually wear my hoodie to give the principal a sign that I need a little help that day. She is always outside when we get off the bus in the morning and she says good morning to every child. She has a smile on her face and some give a high five but we are all happy to see her each and every day. She and all of the other teachers on bus duty tell the kids as they are getting off the bus to "dream big" and they reply "and work hard!" I need to work hard because I know one day I am going to be able to wear clean clothes and have my refrigerator stocked with a lot of food.

I wear my hoodie not to be defiant or mean but because it shields me and covers up my shame. I don't know why my teacher got upset with me because my hoodie was up but from that day forward she never said anything about my hoodie.

Fact: *Kids come through the school door every day and they are doing their best. One teacher, one principal, one adult is all that a child needs.*

Generational poverty is a cycle that is hard to break but I do believe people try their best and give it their all but it is so hard to break down that wall.

When a child comes into the school and they are not clean or have lice, and who is sometimes mean, know that the caretaker is not always making good choices but they need some help. We can reach out to give them some help but what is most important is that the child sees they are special day in and day out.

Don't assume that no one cares, sometimes life just isn't fair. We are all born into this world pretty much the same way but opportunity for each baby that is born is not always fair. If we are all servants of mankind we can help level the playing field and leave no one behind.

Chapter Five
The Camouflage Hoodie
(Body Image & Self-Esteem)

CAMOUFLAGE

HOODIE

I don't look like the rest of the kids. My body is unlike the magazine bodies that you see. I have rolls over my jeans and my face is broken out. Other kids call me names. They watch what I eat and this causes me shame.

I am in sixth grade and the rest of the kids are older and they point and snicker and make fun of my belly. I go to the gym and it's the worst part of the day because I have to dress out and I can't cover myself.

My hoodie camouflages it all, no one can see how big or how small.
If I have gained more weight, they don't know.
They are going to be mean no matter where I go.

I want to look better and care about myself but when I get home there is only junk food in the house.
I am starving because I can't eat at school because of the snarky remarks I just keep to myself and don't look up for this gives them the power to continue with their remarks.

I try to let it go but it builds up inside and now I feel anxious and so out of control.
My heart beats fast as I walk into the room because I can't sit at the desk. There is just no room.

I read a lot so I go to the library and find books on health and begin to make wiser choices no matter what's in the house.
I talk to my mom and tell her I don't want to wear this hoodie anymore.

I want to wear cool clothes that make me feel good.
We talk about healthy food and exercise and we go outside more sundown to sunrise.

Soon the weight begins to disappear and my mom and I make healthier choices because we care.
Living behind a hoodie is hard and unfair.
Why can't we accept each other for who we really are?

I want to be a chef someday and focus on teenagers to show them the way. To hold their head up high and teach them to be themselves no matter what others say.
We can all change and be who we want to be but don't do it for others, do it for yourself.

Be kind to yourself and talk about your feelings and know that you are beautiful no matter what everyone else may say.
You are here for a reason and you are here to stay.

No more hoodies no matter the weight.
Be yourself and be kind.
That is all that matters.
Remember the magazines have been photoshopped and easily influence young people's minds.
Don't let them fool you, be wiser and true to yourself and be bold, stand up, and be proud of yourself.

You have every right to be here.
You are loved and you are kind.
There will always be kids who are hurtful and blind.

Blind to the beauty that you hold.
Your love and your kindness are the true gifts of your soul.
The magazines, social media, are all a distraction and it may not
seem real now but none of that matters.

I promise you if you love yourself others will love you too and no
matter what our bodies look like we are all going to get old and
wrinkly like our grammas and grampas but isn't it a waste to be
worried about rolls and how our pants look and fit.
You don't have time for that.
Enjoy every day.
Don't compare yourself to others.

You are one of a kind.
    A gem.
        A diamond like no other.
            Be yourself, be kind, and love one another.

Fact: Body Dysmorphic Disorder (BDD) is a mental health condition where a person is overly preoccupied with thinking about their body in comparison with what they believe it should look like. This type of thought process can lead to very unhealthy behaviors for boys and girls. Social media advertisements and celebrity news play a lot in this problem. One of the most important things is to talk to your child and let them know that all of our bodies go through changes every day and one of the most important things to do is make sure you are healthy.

Involving the whole family in healthy eating habits and activities that you love or want to learn are two ways to focus on health not on how you look. Encourage children to get outside and play. Go for walks, hike, bike, any movement at all helps to support a healthy heart.

Whether you are a parent, teacher, grandparent, or caregiver, limit sedentary activities such as video games, and computers to no more than one hour a day. Schools play a vital role in the lack of activity. Students should not sit or be on computers for long periods of time. Monitor how long your child is on a computer and slowly wean them off. To just cut it out is too big of a move. Slow and steady wins the race.

There are a lot of health problems that youth are facing today that they have never faced. Type 2 diabetes, joint problems, breathing concerns, and high cholesterol are on the rise. Talk to your child about healthy choices. Make meals together and you may have to check with your doctor if you are concerned. Most of all never make your child feel bad about his/her weight and don't push your child to exercise. Try to make it as natural as you can, have fun and enjoy healthy eating.

Chapter 6
The Rainbow Hoodie
(Gender Identity)

HOODIE

Gay, straight, lesbian, non-binary or bi–
He- She- They- and We-
We know they wonder WHY!

Sometimes I don't know why–
    WHY it matters to them
        WHY it matters to me

I just want to be free
Free to be who I am
Free to not have to take a stand.

To be respected and not feel like I have to explain myself
but just to feel real with no shame.

My hoodies are bright–red, yellow, blue, purple, and green.
My hair matches it with bright hues of blue on my bleached
blonde hair.

I know everyone thinks that I don't care.
But I do care, especially when they stare.

I pull myself together and I get up and go. Every day is hard but I
need to grow.
I need to be myself, no matter what they say.

I can't live in shame because they can't deal.
I need to be who I am so I can feel.

I put on my mask and everyone thinks I am okay
Reality is, I'm just gay.

I shouldn't have to explain my sexuality. Do boys who like girls have
to say it out loud? We should be able to blend in and be who we are,
love who we want, and be happy and content.

We talk about it constantly like it's a bad thing. They say something
is wrong and we should have shame. I care about people and see us
all the same. I am strong and proud and I believe in everyone's right
to be who they are without a fight.

It's so hard to be who I am
Not because I am ashamed but I am just tired of the fight.

We can't have our own
bathroom, but why do we
need our own bathrooms? We
all need our privacy even if
we're not gay-it's just that this
is the way we all respect each
other.

Whether you're a brother or
a sister, a he, she, we, they or me. All of this is private. So why can't
they just stop talking, humiliating, bad-mouthing, disrespecting, and
throwing a fit?

We all want the same thing–we want and deserve respect.
We want to be ourselves.

We want to love who we want to love.
We want to be friends with who we want to be friends with.

We are just like YOU–YOU–and YOU. Look in the mirror, we're not different don't you see? We have feelings, we care, and we want to be seen.

Instead–we can't wear our hoods, we have to conform, no matter how much they say we are all equal, they still make us less than and not more.

Why can't I be me?
Why must they stop and stare?

I just thought everyone is the same and we all have rights.

We should be allowed to stand up tall. To laugh. To cry. To be ALL. We are trying so hard to be accepted by fellow students, teachers, society, and all.

Get to know us. We care. We are nice.
We have fun. We sing. We shout. We are worth the time to get to know us, come check us out.

Close your eyes if you must, talk to us, and get to know us.

Fact: *Helping our youth navigate their gender identity or sexual orientation can sometimes be a difficult hurdle for parents. Before we go any further the first thing is to know your child is no different, no better, no worse, they are just trying to answer questions that they may have.*

It is common for all kids to question their gender identity or sexual orientation. When the child feels supported by their family they will do their best. To navigate these waters alone or to be ridiculed can lead to emotional harm or worse for our young children.

Today it is more and more common to hear about kids questioning their identity (what gender they feel they are) or their sexual orientation (who they are attracted to).

Again, many teachers, grandparents, or parents have trouble either understanding or knowing what to do when their child is questioning. Agreeing or not agreeing with your child is something that you may need to work through but remember this is about your child. Letting them know you love them no matter what, that you accept them, and that you will always be there to protect them in every way you know how.

Your child may have a very hard time telling you so you may want to broach the conversation and say, "so, I notice that you are wearing makeup and your outfits have changed." Then let your child talk and you listen. Taking the opposition approach is never what is best. Using slurs or other derogatory statements will not create an atmosphere where the child feels safe to be himself, herself, or themself.

It's never about what we feel or how it makes us feel. It's about helping your child navigate their world and to know that they are loved and cared for no matter what.

Chapter 7
My Hoodie

 HOODIE

I am not sure why this has come to be.
Why are they on my back, can't they see?

I come to school and I do my best to make my mom proud.
She wants me to do better than her and not just go with the crowd.

She got into some bad things that caused her to struggle in her life
and she doesn't want me to have the same strife.

She is a single mom who does her best and wants me to succeed.
She is giving everything to me that she's got to me to make sure I'm
never in need.

My hood was pulled up because of the shame that I felt.
My mom put dreads in my hair and I wanted to pull them out.

Again she tried her best and now I don't look like the rest.

I can get through this by leaving my hood up, I pray.
But knowing my teacher, she is going to have something to say.

I was ok on the bus. I just fit right in and no one said a word.
I sat down and tried to act cool, but my heart was beating so fast we
were almost at school.

I walked in the door and heard the first person say, not good
morning or hello just "get your hood down son, we're in school."

I kept walking and swallowed hard. And telling myself it's ok, you can do this, keep smiling, and act like you didn't hear.
Get into the classroom and go to your seat. Get busy with your morning work and don't look up, but immediately I hear her feet.

"You need to take your hood down, we are in school." I told her I was cold and she sighed heavily and walked away.
She will be back, it's just a deterrent I say.

She reminded us that we would walk across the stage that day so get our speeches out that we will read aloud today.
The speeches we wrote were our vows not to do drugs. It was through a program at our school that I was very proud of.

I knew it meant a lot to my mom because of the life that she led, she wanted great things for me that lay ahead. This was my promise to her and to myself but just before we got to the door I was pulled to the side and told hood down or you're not walking on stage. It's disrespectful, so hood down now, or be on your way.

I knew I couldn't let my mom down but the ridicule I was going to get from the other kids was too much to bear.
I walked over and sat down near my mom but I knew I couldn't say a word right then or I would burst out into tears and run.

My mom tried to talk to me and I felt so bad. I couldn't say a word. I was so mad. I wish I would have told my teacher or I wish someone would have asked. I just needed a few days so my new haircut would pass.

My dreads were so short and looked unkempt and frizzy. My mom told me it could take up to six months depending on how well my hair forms locs. I knew I didn't have that kind of time to wear a hoodie and never look up.

I think I am a pretty good kid and they should know. They are adults. I am not defiant, I just need a friend, a fo.

A friend who knows me and understands this is not me being rebellious but me trying to fit in. So can't they take their rule and make it bend?

I am not sure why this rule exists today. I see people young and old wear hats every day.

The program is over and my mom walks over to the adults and asks why her son was not able to walk.

They shared they asked me to pull down my hood out of respect for the school and for him they said.
They said he chose not to walk. We didn't say to sit out but I had no choice. I felt my back was against the wall and I had to shout.

It looked like I was being bad but I was so hurt. My mom walked me to the car and she was upset. I thought this was only a shirt.

A shirt with a hood that covered my hair, that I was so embarrassed of. I didn't want people to stare.

I got in the car and my mom said this is not like you. I told her why I did what I did and she said she understood and that I was just a kid.

The adults should have asked you just like I did but instead, they stick to a rule that does not help it hurts instead.

My mom called the school when she calmed down and told them this could all have been avoided had they asked her son.

This ceremony meant more to her than anyone could have known. Again, it's just a hood, I wasn't hurting anyone.

Fact: *Schools have rules and as good citizens we should follow but common sense goes a long way. The reality of this story is no one asked the child what was going on. It was out of character for him and they would have learned no malintent was there or need to scorn.*

This will no doubt leave a memory for this mother and this child but I think the bigger lesson here was learned by the school. Relationships and trust are needed in a classroom and in a school. Helping our children maneuver through life is no easy feat but that is a school job and we need to do better.

I know this mother will find the wisdom she needs to help keep her son on track and lead the life that he deserves. There is always good that comes out of bad and this is one of those times. The school learned a valuable lesson about relationships and trust. The student learned that even though he is young his words matter and to talk to an adult. His mom realizes it's not the walk that matters but rather her son not going against his word and he takes a stand. She is raising a strong young man and she should be proud of that.

Chapter Eight

Dear Society, Parents, Grand Parents, Teachers, Administrators, Counselors, and anyone who works with adolescents,

Before you judge kids who wear hoodies, find out the real reasons behind the hood. Some kids wear hoodies just because they like hoodies. For a number of kids, it can be emotional comfort to wear a hoodie. Kids who have anxiety may feel more comfortable wearing a hoodie. Besides the warmth, they feel like they blend in better, and do not stick out.

There are societal biases against adolescents of color when wearing a hoodie. These are the biases that need to disappear. These biases are brought on by the media we watch. When you Google the word hoodie and boys or adults, under images, you will find social media depicting more brown-skinned people wearing hoodies, usually white boys or white men are smiling and brown-skinned people not smiling or look like they are in a more impoverished place. This needs to stop and we need to understand that biases and prejudices are influenced by social media. We need to make our children aware of this. We need to teach children that we are all equal.

Some believe that when a youth has their hoodie pulled up it is seen as a sign of defiance. Getting to know the student and understanding where he or she is coming from is how we reach students and make them feel comfortable in their own skin. Someone once told me there is a story behind every child's behavior. It is our job to understand the story and then help the child move through the behavior to learn a more socially accepted behavior.

Sometimes there are other reasons kids wear hoodies or even long sleeves or long pants even when it's a hundred-degree weather. Don't be alarmed when you see a hoodie. The best way to know is to always have an open relationship with your child or student. Let them always know it is a safe place, you care about them, and that together you can work through any problems or concerns that they have.

Kids wear hoodies for many reasons. The reasons I have found that schools have a policy against hoodies are as follows:

- Deemed unsafe
- Unprofessional
- Disrespectful
- Distraction from learning

I want you to think about the students that are portrayed in this book and none of them had any of the intentions listed above. In all of my interviews, no child shared anything closely related to any of the reasons schools don't allow hoodies.

We need to be open and understanding of our children and allow them to express themselves and we need to also show them that we care by getting to know them. There is always a reason behind every behavior. Believe in our children and show them we care. They will grow up being caring, loving, respectful people if we don't shut them down or turn them away.

*Fact: I have come to know that there is usually a story behind the hood.
Be aware…*

…Care…

…help them feel understood.

Don't be too quick to judge, you may find yourself or your child in the same situation being misunderstood.

Our children are our most precious gifts. Their anger, their joy, their love, and their grace, all come from a place.

Be kind, and try to understand and give guidance,

a smile or a helping hand.

We are all here together for a reason, it is our job to take care of our children.

So whether you are a parent, a grandmother, grandfather, aunt, uncle, or cousin,

a teacher, a preacher, or just someone passing by, lend them a smile and a kind heart and there is no doubt this will be a better world if you play your part.

I know the hoods will come down when we get to know our kids and help them through life's troubles that lie ahead.

This book should by no means be used to diagnose or to be used as a finite understanding of all of the complex social norms with each of these characters. It has been written to shed light on relationships, grace, caring, and most of all the love of mankind.

Every child deserves the best life to live and we as adults should foster and protect them until they are ready to be on their own and sometimes even after that, if they need us. As parents, educators, or caretakers we all are connected in some way by being human beings.

Let's always build relationships, seek to understand, and not condemn. Share one's belief with trust and respect and give each other respect as well.

I write this book because I, like many of you, see myself as living a life of service. My life's work has been dedicated to children. There has been nothing as rewarding or as important in my mind as the happiness of children.

I watch day in and day out how when a child is born into this world they are not born with all of the things they need much less the things they deserve. I have often witnessed the importance of an adult or a friend of the child who changes the child's life forever.

We are but one caring adult away from the success story of a child. Be that caring adult.

May we always do what is best for children.

"A life lived in service is not a sacrifice but an honor."

~ Queen Elizabeth

Support

Anxiety: Banana Moon makes a hoodie to help people with anxiety. The Hoodie has several sensory tools such as a tactile infinity circle, fidget, weighted pockets, and more.

https://www.banana-moon-clothing.co.uk/personalised-clothing/unisex/hoodies/anti-anxiety-hoodie-2584

Autism: There is no one type of autism. From What is Autism to the Parents Guide to Autism can be found here:

https://www.autismspeaks.org/what-autism

Low socioeconomic or generational poverty: Salvation Army

https://www.salvationarmyusa.org/usn/the-lgbtq-community-and-the-salvation-army/

References

Center for Teaching by Patricia Armstrong Bloom's Taxonomy
https://cft.vanderbilt.edu/guides-sub-pages/blooms-taxonomy/

Cleveland Clinic How To Support Your Child as They Explore
Their Gender Identity
https://health.clevelandclinic.org/think-your-child-might-be-
questioning-their-gender-identity

Maslow's Hierarchy of Needs
https://www.simplypsychology.org/maslow.html
By Saul Mcleod, PhD Updated on November 24, 2023

Body dysmorphic disorder Mayo Clinic
https://www.mayoclinic.org/diseases-conditions/
body-dysmorphic-disorder/symptoms-causes/syc-20353938

Autism Speaks
https://www.autismspeaks.org/?form=donate&utm_
medium=paidsearch&utm_source=bing&utm_campaign=IS-
branded-conv&utm_content=IS-evergreen&msclkid=44b4dda6a2c
7112ed8cdb82b4b843950

Generational Poverty Understanding and Working with Students
and Adults from Poverty
https://www.ahaprocess.com/wp-content/uploads/2013/09/
Understanding-Poverty-Ruby-Payne-Poverty-Series-I-IV.pdf

Milton Keynes UK
Ingram Content Group UK Ltd.
UKHW020208110324
439151UK00007B/125